IN ON IT

IN ON IT

Daniel MacIvor

In On It
first published 2001 by
Scirocco Drama
An imprint of J. Gordon Shillingford Publishing Inc.
© 2001 Daniel MacIvor

Scirocco Drama Series Editor: Glenda MacFarlane
Cover design by Doowah Design Inc.
Author and cover photo by Guntar Kravis
Printed and bound in Canada

We acknowledge the financial support of The Canada Council for the Arts and the
Manitoba Arts Council for our publishing program.

Canadian Cataloguing in Publication Data

MacIvor, Daniel, 1962-
        In on it

A play.
ISBN 1-896239-81-1

        I. Title.

PS8575.I86I6 2001   C812'.54   C2001-901106-7
PR9199.3.M322516 2001

J. Gordon Shillingford Publishing
P.O. Box 86, 905 Corydon Avenue, Winnipeg, MB Canada R3M 3S3

For

David Newhouser and Julie Fox

Special Thanks

To Kimberly Purtell, Richard Feren, Sherrie Johnson and especially Darren O'Donnell for their generous and insightful dramaturgical input during the development of this text.

Daniel MacIvor

Daniel MacIvor has been creating theatre since 1986. He is a writer, performer, director, producer and artistic director of da da kamera. His plays include *See Bob Run, Wild Abandon, Never Swim Alone, 2-2 Tango, House, Here Lies Henry, The Soldier Dreams* and *Monster*. His plays have toured extensively throughout Canada, the United States, Israel, the United Kingdom, and Australia.

Production History

In On It was produced by da da kamera and premiered at the Vancouver East Cultural Centre in January, 2001, with the following cast:

THIS ONE .... Daniel MacIvor
THAT ONE .... Darren O'Donnell

Written and directed by Daniel MacIvor
Sound and music designed and operated by Richard Feren
Lighting operated and co-designed by Kimberly Purtell
Technical Direction by Kimberly Purtell
Produced by Sherrie Johnson

A commission of the Vancouver East Cultural Centre.

This project could not have happened without the following development partners: Festival Antigonish (Antigonish, NS, Canada), Traverse Theatre (Edinburgh, Scotland), Philadelphia Fringe Festival (Philadelphia, PA, USA), Studio Theatre (Washington, DC, USA), High Performance Rodeo (Calgary, AB, Canada) and the Vancouver East Cultural Centre (Vancouver, BC, Canada).

Notes on the Play

In On It has three distinct realities (which can and do overlap and fishtail); they are: The Play, The Show and The Past. The Play is the story of Ray—more often than not there is a sense of this happening in a highly theatrical, artificial environment; The Show: which is happening now, here, tonight and mainly consists of THIS ONE and THAT ONE discussing the Play and its development and then eventually their relationship and it's development; and The Past which consists of This One and That One meeting and becoming lovers.

Notes on Design

We travelled to many theatres during the development and touring of *In On It*, and our design concept was to strip each of these theatres to the bare walls and use only two chairs. These were mostly simple stacking chairs with metal frames and fabric-covered seats and backs—if they weren't already black, we'd spray-paint the frames matte black and cover the backs and seats with black fabric. The point was to create a neutral feeling—not to expect the chairs to convey the personality of either of the characters, or suggest anything about their life together.

The only props used were the two chairs, a grey sports jacket, a tissue, a poster, and a set of keys. The jacket and chairs are carefully tracked in the script, based on many months of development and performance.

The stage itself had five different lighting states:
—**The Play State** (in which the "Play" would take place)
A grid of six specials; a character would enter into or be discovered in one of the specials.

—**The Show State** (where This One and That One assess the development of the "Play")
A large box of light, clearly defined on the floor, in which This One and That One could move freely. Sometimes this box would hit the back wall, creating a kind of proscenium of light; this often gave us more freedom of movement with fewer lights, but it very much depended on the shape of the back wall and the depth of the space.
—**The Past State**
A long thin bar of light (also clearly defined on the floor), in which This One and That One had a much more restricted range of motion.
—**Hybrid State** (created for That One's monologues and for the "Telephone Call") tight specials
—**Performance State**
Full bright light which illuminated the stage and the walls around it, and sometimes even the ceiling.

The only blackouts were as indicated in the script.

The only props used were the two chairs, a grey sports jacket, a tissue and a set of keys.

The jacket and the two chairs are carefully tracked in the script based on many months of development and performance.

Notes on Style

In order to clearly delineate between the three realities in *In On It* we developed three different kind of "styles" (in the most superficial sense) of acting.

In the **Play** we would both perform out—to the audience—but react as if we were actually facing one another. (The script is written with this as an assumed style so that a stage direction like *BRENDA turns to RAY* indicates that the actor playing Brenda turns away from the audience and faces the other actor.)

In the **Show** we would maintain an awareness of the audience, stage directions indicate when we addressed the audience.

In the **Past** we would suddenly be inside a fourth-wall reality with no awareness of the audience whatsoever.

Notes on Story

The back story we had for *In On It* was as follows: Brad is killed in a head-on collision with a blue Mercedes driven by a man named Raymond King. There is some question as to how this accident happened; there seemed to be no reason for the car to veer into Brad's lane. In order to give some reason for this "accident" (and to assuage his guilt for insisting that Brad drive his car that day) Brian creates the play about Ray, his suicide and the reasons for it. Brad in effect is returning "from the dead" to assist in the creation of the play (and show) on this evening. This story was valuable for the actors but it was not necessary that the audience "get" this story—the audience will get the story they need to get.

And finally:

In the script the characters are called Brad and Brian although they never refer to one another by name. This is so that the actors understand they are playing real characters and not some stylized version of such. It is very important that in any program listing for any future production of this play that the characters be listed as THIS ONE and THAT ONE—this is how each refers to the other—in this way the audience slowly comes to realize that these characters are not post-modern simulations. This helps to keep the audience guessing as to the nature of the play and causes them to continually re-evaluate their perception of such.

Pre-show: A bare space brightly lit. Two simple black chairs sit side by side upstage left. A jacket lies centre stage as if having been casually dropped there. As pre-show music we hear a collection of Lesley Gore songs. The final song of the preshow is "Sunshine Lollipops." With the final beat of this song, the house and stage are plunged into darkness leaving only the jacket lit by a tight special. We sit in silence with this image for several seconds until:

We hear Maria Callas singing an aria from the mad scene of "Anna Bolena" by Donazetti. In the darkness we see the form of a man in a white (or light-coloured) shirt and a tie. He slowly enters from offstage. This is BRIAN. BRIAN approaches the jacket. He stands looking down at it. Slowly he picks up the jacket puts it on. As he adjusts the jacket, we hear the beginning of screeching tires. The aria is brutally interrupted by a shriek. Light snaps to a special on BRIAN as he looks up at the audience. He addresses the audience.

BRIAN: There are the things that happen out of careful planning: two people have a wedding, someone builds a boat, a person writes a play. The things that happen around guest lists and blueprints and re-writes. And then there are the things that happen over which we have no control. The things that sneak up on us. The things that just happen. The arbitrary optional life-changing things that seem to make no sense; the things we have to invent sense for. Lots of things. Little things: the music our lover listens to; bigger things: the way our health can come out from under us like a carpet on a hardwood floor; huge things: the blue Mercedes.

I can only imagine it but when I do, it's like this: You're on the road doing some errands, you've got to exchange some tickets, pick up a prescription for somebody's migraine, the usual. You pull out onto the highway to save some time, in your big powerful fast machine, being come at by a lot of other big powerful fast machines, driven by people about whose level of mental health or blood alcohol you know nothing. That's a sobering thought; you go for the radio. Crap. Crap. More crap. Crap. Something familiar. Crap. Back to something familiar. Can't find it. Where was it? One-oh-one point what? Or? Before the sports after the metal. There it is! And in that tiny moment of taking your attention ever so briefly away from the big machine in your hands, the other guy veers into your lane and you look up just in time to see the headlights of the blue Mercedes.

BRAD speaks from the darkness. The light slowly shifts from BRIAN's special into the SHOW state.

BRAD: Do you think that's a good way to start?

BRAD enters from the darkness and stands just on the edge of the light.

Do you think that's a good way to start?

BRIAN: Start what?

BRAD enters the light.

BRAD: The show.

BRIAN: It's not a show, it's a play.

BRIAN steps upstage and picks up one of the chairs. He carries it downstage.

BRAD: Oh. *(To audience.)* Hi *(To an individual.)* Hey!

BRIAN: Are you here to help or...?

BRAD: Oh. Sure. Sorry.

BRIAN places the chair downstage centre facing the audience.

BRIAN: Now we can start.

BRAD: Haven't we started?

BRIAN takes off the jacket and offers it to BRAD. BRAD takes the jacket and puts it on.

BRIAN: Now we're starting.

BRIAN steps away and takes up a position upstage right facing the audience. BRAD sits in the chair.

Light snaps to PLAY state (two specials.) BRIAN is the DOCTOR. BRAD is RAY.

SOUND of a muted heartbeat which continues throughout.

DOCTOR: Good morning Ray.

RAY: Good morning Doc.

DOCTOR: How was your weekend?

RAY: Fine. You know, considering.

DOCTOR: Considering?

RAY: I haven't been sleeping.

DOCTOR: Really?

RAY: Just nerves and...dreams. Lots of dreams. I keep having this dream about a concrete boat. I'm on this boat—big type, you know, big like a ship practically. And it's floating on like a kind of a canal and it's made of concrete. Concrete blocks, concrete slabs. I keep thinking it should sink—but it doesn't. It's vaguely unnerving. What do you make of that?

DOCTOR: Well…

RAY: Dreaming about concrete boats.

DOCTOR: Not my beat really.

RAY: What's that?

DOCTOR: Not my major.

RAY: Right.

DOCTOR: But there are books, you know, dream, you know, dictionaries…

RAY: Right.

DOCTOR: Do you have a boat?

RAY: No.

DOCTOR: Maybe it means you should get a boat.

RAY: Should I?

DOCTOR: How's Brenda?

RAY: Good. She's thinking about going back to school.

DOCTOR: Oh yeah?

RAY: She never got her degree. Really just something to do. She also started going back to church. Which is I guess something that happens at a certain age. Or…I guess.

DOCTOR: And is Miles still in school?

RAY: No he's out, he's working.

DOCTOR: In?

RAY: Advertising.

DOCTOR: Advertising? Really? A professional.

RAY: I know. It seems like just last year I was teaching him how to ride a bicycle and now he's beating me at squash.

DOCTOR: That's the way. And your Dad is settled in all right at the home?

RAY: Oh yeah. And the car's running fine and the weed killer's working.

DOCTOR: Ha ha ha.

RAY: How am I?

DOCTOR: Can I get you something?

            Sound: the heart beat accelerates.

RAY: Sorry?

DOCTOR: Can Eileen get you something?

RAY: What do you mean?

DOCTOR: A glass of water or…?

RAY: Oh. No. Thank you. No.

DOCTOR: Raymond.

RAY: What?

DOCTOR: I've been looking over your test results. There's nothing conclusive—we're going to need some more tests before we can say what's really going on.

RAY: What might be going on?

DOCTOR: We're looking at a number of possibilities.

RAY: Ranging from?

DOCTOR: I'm concerned.

RAY: You're concerned.

DOCTOR: I'd like to get you into the hospital for a couple of days.

RAY: The hospital?

DOCTOR: The tests are quite extensive.

RAY: When?

DOCTOR: This week if we can manage it.

RAY: Right away?

DOCTOR: That would be best yes.

RAY: Oh. Oh. Oh. What are you telling me?

DOCTOR: We're looking a number of possibilities.

RAY: Worst case scenario?

DOCTOR: I can't—

RAY: Am I sick?

DOCTOR: Ray. It's like this—you've got to stay strong and you've got to stay positive. That's your job.

RAY: Oh my God.

DOCTOR: As for the sleeping I can give you something if you like.

RAY: Oh my God.

DOCTOR: Can I get you a glass of water?

RAY: Oh my God.

DOCTOR: We don't know anything yet.

RAY: Who's "we"?

DOCTOR: Sorry?

RAY: "We don't know anything yet." Who's "we"?

DOCTOR: Uh… You and I.

RAY: Bullshit. Of course I don't know anything. I'm not supposed to know anything, that's how this works. I'm not part of your "we". Who's "we"? You and who? You and the entire medical profession? You and all the healthy people? You and Eileen? She's stupid, you know. Did you know she was stupid? You have a stupid receptionist. She can't remember my name. I've been coming longer than she's been working here and she can't remember my name. That's just stupidity. Or malice. But she doesn't appear bright enough to be malicious.

DOCTOR: Raymond you're upset it's perfectly under-standable.

RAY: You're enjoying this aren't you?

DOCTOR: Pardon me?

RAY: You are. You love this. You get to play "Doctor". That's what this is all about isn't it?

DOCTOR: (Slight nervous laughter.) Ray. Let's just take a step back from this for a second shall we?

RAY: Look at you, you are loving this, you're laughing.

DOCTOR: I'm not—Ray, you're upset, it's normal.

RAY: Oh shut up. Who do you think you are? Marcus Welby? George Fucking Clooney?

DOCTOR: Okay Raymond.

RAY: And what's the white coat supposed to signify? How ridiculous. What, did you just come in from the lab? Who's the white coat for? The pert little stupid bitch receptionist out front?

            Sound: the heartbeat is at its most rapid. Note: BRIAN's white- or light-coloured shirt represents the lab coat—there should be no actual lab coat.

DOCTOR: Mister King.

RAY: You're pathetic. I bet you wear it outside. I bet you plan little excursions to the coffee shop just so you can wear it in the street. Watching yourself in the windows. Aren't you something. God, I pity you. You're a fool.

             Silence. Sound: the heartbeat returns to normal.

DOCTOR: Can I get you a glass of water?

RAY: Yes please.

             BRIAN steps away from the DOCTOR's spot.

             Sound out and light snaps to SHOW state. BRIAN heads for the chair upstage left.

BRAD: How was that?

             BRIAN stops in his tracks.

BRIAN: What?

BRAD: How was that?

BRIAN: How was that how?

BRAD: How was I as Ray?

             BRIAN regards the audience briefly.

BRIAN: I'm don't think this is really the time to be talking about it.

             BRIAN moves upstage and retrieves the second chair. He places it upstage right facing the audience.

BRAD: I'm just asking. Was the task fulfilled?

BRIAN: The task?

BRAD: Yeah.

BRIAN: Yes whatever.

BRAD: Okay then, I'll just keep doing what I'm doing.

BRIAN: Um.

BRAD: Yes?

BRIAN: It's just that it's not that Ray's angry.

BRAD rises, BRIAN takes the chair BRAD has been sitting in and places it upstage stage left facing the audience.

BRAD: He's not angry.

BRIAN: No.

BRAD: He's raving.

BRIAN: He's not raving.

BRAD: "George Fucking Clooney."

BRIAN: So?

BRIAN sits in the stage left chair he has just placed.

BRAD: "Pert little stupid bitch—"

BRIAN: No I know but—

BRAD: How else then?

BRAD takes off his jacket and offers it to BRIAN.

How else?

BRIAN considers the audience a moment, he then takes the jacket from BRAD and puts it on as he crosses to the stage right chair. BRAD takes up a position ready to sit in the stage left chair. BRIAN takes up a position ready to sit in the stage right chair. It is during this putting on of the jacket that BRIAN—unseen by the audience—takes a tissue from the pocket of the jacket and palms it in his left hand.

BRAD: Like this.

          Light snaps to PLAY state—one special only on
          BRAD.

          Sound: a busy restaurant at lunchtime.

          BRAD speaks as he sits. He is now MILES.

MILES: Dad? Sorry I'm late. Damn rain. Dad? Ray?

          Light snaps to PLAY state special on BRIAN.

          BRIAN speaks as he sits. He is now RAY.

RAY: Oh. Miles. Yes. Hi. Sorry.

MILES: Sorry I'm late.

RAY: Not a problem.

MILES: Damn rain.

RAY: Yeah.

MILES: It was supposed to be sunny.

RAY: Was it?

MILES: Damn weathermen don't know a damn thing.
          They probably pick the damn forecast out of a
          damn hat. So I don't bring an umbrella this
          morning and now I've got to buy another—and
          we've got half a dozen at home.

RAY: Well you know.

MILES: Have you ordered? Dad?

RAY: What?

MILES: Have you ordered?

RAY: Oh. No.

MILES: The tortellini's terrible, the eggplant's soggy, the
          catch of the day is frozen and the specials aren't.

RAY: Miles?

MILES: Yeah?

RAY: How's work?

MILES: A farce. You know what Blanchard says to me this morning? "We've got to make plastic fun again." What? Hello? Fun? The old coot's got us some major plastics manufacturer as a client—no other agency in the western hemisphere would touch them no doubt. The world is ten minutes away from toxic implosion, skateboarders are running multi-nationals, the right is about to embrace hemp as the new miracle fibre and he wants to make plastic fun again. Anyways people aren't interested in fun anymore, people are interested in function. Oh, the veal's not awful.

RAY: I saw the Doctor yesterday, I have to go for some tests.

MILES: Yeah? I've got a mole I should get looked at. Does that look normal to you? Actually it looks fine in here—it's probably just the ridiculous bulbs in the damn bathroom. Julie insists on the lowest wattage she can find—what is that, twenty or something? In terms of aging she's of the opinion that if you can't see it it ain't happening. Oh yeah hey, we've got tickets for the opera at the conservatory next week and we can't use them. I know Mom was talking about it. Do you think you guys would be into it? I'd love to but Julie's got her book club. I don't know why she doesn't write this stuff down. Well I mean she does but... Okay what is this? She pretends to make lists. Okay, I mean she makes the lists but she never looks at them again—I mean she never consults them again—never scratches anything off them. What is that? That is not a list. That is just a piece of paper with words on it. A list needs to be updated, altered, checked. That's what makes it a list. And she keeps losing them. I know because I keep finding them. I mean I'm sorry but there are the kind of people who make lists and the kind of people who lose things—these are mutually exclusive qualities. I mean "Let's face the facts, Julie!" You know? "Let's live in the damn world, Julie."

RAY drops his head and begins to weep.

Dad? What's going on? Dad? Stop it. For God's sake. Dad, you're making a scene.

RAY: I'm sick.

MILES: What?

RAY: I'm sick.

MILES: No you're not, stop it.

RAY: I have to go into the hospital.

MILES: For what?

RAY: For tests.

MILES: Tests. Tests are just tests. People go for tests all the time.

RAY: I'm sick.

MILES: How sick?

RAY: They don't know.

MILES: Yeah, well, tests, see. Tests. Then they find the thing then they test the thing then they fix the thing. Dad? Right? Come on. Here.

> *MILES raises his empty left hand toward the audience. RAY raises his left hand toward the audience and reveals the tissue he has been palming—the effect being that MILES has handed RAY a tissue.*

You're all mucousy.

Silence.

How come Mom didn't call me?

RAY: I didn't tell your Mother yet.

MILES: Well who'd you tell?

RAY: Nobody. Just you.

MILES: You told me first? Why'd you tell me first? Don't be telling me stuff like this first. I'm no good with stuff like this. Don't tell me this stuff first okay.

RAY: Sorry.

MILES: That's okay but just…you know.

RAY: Sorry.

MILES: Tell Mom. Don't tell Mom you told me. Just tell Mom. Tell Mom you told her first. She'd want you to, you know, tell her first. Tell her first and then she'll call me and I'll talk to Mom and then everything will be okay. Okay? Okay Dad?

RAY: Okay.

MILES: Should we have a drink? Do you want a drink?

RAY: Sure.

MILES: I'm a little hungry. How are you? Are you hungry?

RAY: I could eat.

MILES: I'm pretty hungry.

RAY: How's the veal?

MILES: Excellent.

MILES looks out the window.

Damn!

RAY: What?

MILES: It stopped raining! And I already bought a damn
            umbrella.

            Sound: fades out.

            *An uncomfortable pause. BRIAN rises. Light snaps
            to SHOW state.*

BRAD: *(To audience.)* It doesn't end very well.

BRIAN: *(To BRAD.)* What?

BRAD: Nothing. And you got an opera thing in there.

BRIAN: Yes.

BRAD: So we'll be expecting a bit of opera? Beyond what
            we've already had?

BRIAN: Problem?

BRAD: No.

BRIAN: Good.

BRAD: So why is Julie such an idiot?

BRIAN: Julie?

BRAD: The wife.

BRIAN: Yeah I know—What about her?

BRAD: She's basically an idiot.

BRIAN: Not necessarily.

BRAD: We never meet her, do we?

BRIAN: No.

BRAD: All we've got to go on is what Miles says about her?

BRIAN: So?

BRAD: So.

BRIAN: So.

BRAD: So basically she's an idiot.

BRIAN: I don't see that.

BRAD: What does Julie represent?

BRIAN: Julie's not important, she's a secondary character.

BRAD: But she must represent something.

BRIAN: No.

BRAD: And what about Elaine?

BRIAN: Who?

BRAD: Elaine the secretary.

BRIAN: Eileen.

BRAD: Eileen yeah.

BRIAN: The receptionist.

BRAD: And she's what? Stupid?

BRIAN: What are you getting at?

BRAD: Nothing, just…not long on positive women.

BRIAN: Pardon me?

BRAD: Nothing, just some people might think you have a problem with women.

BRIAN: I don't have a problem with women.

BRAD: I'm not saying you do, I'm just saying—

BRIAN: If anyone has a problem with women you have a problem with women.

BRAD: I do?

BRIAN: Yes.

BRAD: In what way?

BRIAN: In lots of ways.

BRAD: For example?

BRIAN: For example... When Kate brought...what's her name over to meet us...

BRAD: Emma?

BRIAN: No.

BRAD: Laura?

BRIAN: No the one with the tattoos and the thing in her nose.

BRAD: Gwen.

BRIAN: Gwen. When Kate brought Gwen over to meet us *(To the audience.)* We're having dinner and... And That One starts talking about...wetness.

BRAD: About what?

BRIAN: Wetness.

             BRIAN picks up the chair he had been sitting in and places it upstage far stage right facing stage left.

BRAD: *(To audience.)* Female ejaculation.

BRIAN: Yes and that sort of thing yes.

BRAD: I think it kind of turned her on actually.

BRIAN: Oh that's sweet.

BRAD: What's so potentially offending about it?

BRIAN: Oh come on.

BRAD: No really.

             BRAD rises. BRIAN approaches BRAD and picks up the chair BRAD had been sitting in. He places it upstage (far stage right) beside the other chair.

BRIAN: You don't know where a person comes from, what their particular experiences are, how they're affected by things.

BRAD: It's just a conversation.

BRIAN: She may have been a Christian.

BRAD: Christians ejaculate.

BRIAN: She might have had issues.

BRAD: Like what?

BRIAN: Like whatever.

BRAD: You are so status quo.

BRIAN: What does that mean?

BRAD: You're dealing with things around this idea of "men are like this" and "women are like this" which quickly devolves into—

BRIAN: Oh please.

BRAD: That "Asians are like this" and "First Nations people are like this."

BRIAN: Here we go.

BRAD: The point is, if you're presenting women as bimbos and half-wits then you are just preserving the status quo which always presents women as bimbos and half-wits. I shouldn't have to tell you this.

BRIAN: You shouldn't have to tell me this?

BRAD: No just... Sorry.

                BRIAN takes off the jacket hand present it to
                BRAD.

BRIAN: Brenda's not a half-wit.

                BRAD takes the jacket and puts it on.

BRAD: She's terrible to Ray.

                BRAD and BRIAN take up positions downstage left
                and right facing out.

BRIAN: Everybody's terrible to Ray, that's the point.

                Light snap to PLAY state (two specials).

                Sound: distant opera on the radio.

                BRIAN is BRENDA, BRAD is RAY.

                Note: In becoming BRENDA, BRIAN crosses one
                arm over his chest and holds his other arm to his
                throat. By doing this BRIAN is doing two things:
                giving BRENDA a sense of feminine elegance and
                also hiding his tie.

RAY: Brenda?

BRENDA: You're late.

RAY: I had a late lunch with Miles.

BRENDA: How's Miles?

RAY: Fine. He says he has some tickets for that thing at
                the conservatory—if you were interested—
                something you wanted to see?

BRENDA: Oh the Puccini.

RAY: I guess.

BRENDA: I read it was overstated.

RAY: Overstated?

BRENDA: Broad strokes. Lacking in subtlety.

RAY: Oh.

BRENDA: Apparently some Latin American director set it in a fish factory or a fruit farm or something.

RAY: Have you been drinking?

BRENDA: Oh shut up Ray.

RAY: Sorry.

            Silence.

RAY: Brenda? We need to talk.

BRENDA: Yes we do, I know we do, this is ridiculous, why do we bother, why do we even try, well we don't, that's just it isn't it, we don't try, we say we will, and with the best intentions, the best intentions, but we don't. I look at you Ray and I feel... *(Long sigh.)* ...love I guess. But it's static, it's dormant, there's nothing moving in here but...concern for you. And the longer I live like this the less I care. I'm calling it quits.

RAY: Brenda can I say something? I really need to say something.

BRENDA: I'm having an affair.

RAY: What?

BRENDA: With Terry Burke.

RAY: Who's Terry Burke?

BRENDA: Pam Ellis's husband.

RAY: Who's Pam Ellis?

BRENDA: Lloyd's mother.

RAY: Terry?

BRENDA: Yes.

RAY: The Christian?

BRENDA: There's nothing wrong with being a Christian Ray.

RAY: Jesus Christ.

BRENDA: Exactly.

RAY: Who am I talking to?

BRENDA: He's a good man.

RAY: And a hypocrite. How long? How long?

BRENDA: Almost a year.

RAY: Oh that's sweet.

BRENDA: He told Pam yesterday—he's spending the day with Lloyd today.

RAY: What?

BRENDA: I'm sorry Ray but my life has opened up, I'm calling it quits. I've packed some things, I'll let you know where I am.

              BRENDA turns to RAY.

              What did you want to say?

              RAY turns to BRENDA.

RAY: Is there such a thing as a concrete boat? Would a concrete boat float? It seems like it wouldn't. It seems like it would just sink.

              BRENDA turns away.

BRENDA: I haven't the slightest idea.

              Silence. BRIAN drops his arms to his sides.

Light snap to SHOW state. Sound out.

BRIAN: See, Brenda's not so bad.

BRAD: She's drunk.

BRIAN: She's not drunk; she's been drinking.

BRAD: She's drunk.

BRIAN: She's upset. She's confused.

BRAD: What's next?

              BRAD and BRIAN exchange positions on the stage.

BRIAN: *(To the audience.)* A beautiful piece of music.

BRAD: Of course.

BRIAN: *(Quietly to BRAD.)* Problem?

BRAD: No.

BRIAN: Fine.

BRAD: Fine.

BRIAN: *(Continuing to audience.)* Maria Callas—

              *Sound: distant Maria Callas which transforms into
              a field: birds, a plane at one point flies distantly
              overhead.*

              —singing the mad scene from Anna Bolena by
              Donzenetti. Anna is on her way to her
              execution; she stops for a moment and in a
              sublime aria recounts the simple joys of her
              childhood.

              BRIAN has taken a position upstage left.

BRAD: And then?

BRIAN: A field. Terry and Lloyd.

BRAD: Can I be Lloyd?

BRIAN: Sure.

BRAD wraps the jacket around his waist.

BRIAN throws an imaginary ball toward the audience.

Light shift to PLAY state.

BRAD becomes LLOYD. BRIAN becomes TERRY.

LLOYD jumps to catch the ball, misses. Chases the ball back and arrives in a special upstage left from where he plays the scene.

LLOYD: Sorry Terry.

(LLOYD throws the ball back.

Note: The two play the scene out, both throwing and catching toward the audience.

Sound: With each catch we hear the sound of the ball hitting a baseball glove. When LLOYD misses the ball we hear it hit the ground and roll along gravel.

You know there's like six billion people on the planet and four point six billion live in abject poverty.

TERRY: Whoa.

TERRY catches the ball, throws it back.

LLOYD: So like twenty percent of the population has eighty percent of the wealth and eighty percent of the population has like twenty percent of the wealth?

LLOYD catches the ball, throws it back.

TERRY: That's quite a bit huh?

TERRY catches the ball, throws it back.

LLOYD: And if you're talking about really really rich people…

LLOYD catches the ball, throws it back.

…there's only like maybe three hundred billionaires on the planet, so hardly any…

TERRY catches the ball, throws it back.

TERRY: Probably fit them all in this field.

LLOYD catches the ball, throws it back.

LLOYD: Yeah and kill them all!

TERRY catches the ball.

TERRY: Hey now…

LLOYD: Just kidding, Terry.

TERRY throws the ball back. LLOYD catches it.

But and plus, um, also there's enough food for everyone in the world—there don't need to be any starving people—

LLOYD throws the ball back.

—it's just that letting food rot is more economically viable for the people who…

TERRY catches the ball.

…the people who…

TERRY throws the ball back; LLOYD catches it.

TERRY: Who make the money off it.

LLOYD: Yeah.

LLOYD throws the ball back. TERRY catches it.

Did you know that one North American produces

more waste than twenty Chinese people?

TERRY throws the ball back. LLOYD misses it.

Sorry Terry.

LLOYD runs out of light to get the ball. TERRY turns so that he is facing LLOYD.

TERRY: You've got a good arm but you can't catch for shit.

LLOYD returns with the ball. He faces TERRY. Until indicated the two speak directly to one another.

LLOYD: What?

TERRY: You've got a good arm.

LLOYD smiles. Silence.

I'm going away.

LLOYD: What?

TERRY: I'm going away.

LLOYD: To Hamilton?

TERRY: No, away away. I'm taking a break. Moving out.

LLOYD: Taking a break?

TERRY: Your Mom and I need some space.

LLOYD: What do you mean?

TERRY: These things just happen Lloyd.

LLOYD: Right.

TERRY: But I just want to say it's been really great hanging out with you the last couple of years. I learned alot of good stuff from you. And hey, it's not like I'm disappearing or anything. I'll be around. We'll stay in touch.

LLOYD: Do you think my Dad might come back?

TERRY: I don't think so.

LLOYD: I didn't think so.

> *LLOYD turns to face out. TERRY turns to face out. THEY continue to throw the ball back and forth as before.*

TERRY: Hey! You know the apostles. Can you name them?

> *LLOYD throws the ball to TERRY.*

LLOYD: John.

TERRY: Good.

> *TERRY throws the ball to LLOYD.*

LLOYD: Peter. Andrew. Matthew.

> *LLOYD throws the ball to TERRY.*

TERRY: That's four.

> *TERRY throws the ball to LLOYD.*

LLOYD: Jacob and Simon.

TERRY: Six.

> *LLOYD throws the ball to TERRY.*

LLOYD: Phillip and Thomas.

TERRY: Eight.

> *TERRY throws the ball to LLOYD.*

LLOYD: Judas.

> *LLOYD throws the ball to TERRY, hard, TERRY almost misses it.*

TERRY: Three more.

TERRY throws the ball to LLOYD.

LLOYD: Thaddeus. Bartholomew.

TERRY: One more.

LLOYD throws the ball to TERRY.

LLOYD: The other Jacob.

TERRY catches the ball and holds on to it.

TERRY: Jacob what?

LLOYD: Jacob Alphonse?

TERRY: No! Jacob Alpheus. But see, you learned some good stuff hanging out with me too.

TERRY throws the ball to LLOYD. LLOYD does not even try to catch it. The ball hits the ground. Silence.

LLOYD: It's not like you were my real Dad or anything anyway.

TERRY: No.

The two stand in silence for a moment.

THEY step downstage, out of the light.

After a moment: Light snaps to SHOW state.

BRAD: That's sad.

BRIAN: That's life.

BRIAN steps across the stage toward the chairs.

BRAD: So Terry...he's only in the one scene?

BRIAN stops.

BRIAN: Yeah.

BRAD: I see.

BRIAN: What?

BRAD: No, no, nothing.

BRIAN: It's not about Terry.

BRAD: I know but just...what purpose does Terry serve? I mean other than for you to explore your abandonment issues.

BRIAN: No no no no no. Terry represents an idea of God.

BRAD: Oh.

BRIAN: As Lloyd will come to later.

BRAD: Oh.

BRIAN: *(To the audience.)* It's complex.

BRAD: Right. So nobody's happy?

BRIAN: Simplistically, yes, I guess.

BRAD: Nobody nobody.

BRIAN: Nobody nobody?

BRAD: Nobody everybody.

BRIAN: That would seem to be the case, yes.

BRAD: Not you, not me.

BRIAN: We had our moments.

BRAD: But not happy?

BRIAN: No.

Sound: Lesley Gore's "Sunshine, Lollipops."

BRAD and BRIAN look at one another through the first verse of the song. BRIAN steps away toward the chairs up stage right. Light slowly shifts to a special on BRAD as the sound falls into the background.

BRAD addresses the audience.

BRAD: How we met. Our friend Kate was having a Commitment Ceremony. This One knows Kate from forever. I know Kate from this lefty book store Kate and I used to work at. And as part of this Commitment Ceremony Kate wants all her friends—instead of bringing gifts—to do some kind of performance—because she's into that sort of thing. And she wants me to do a dance to this Lesley Gore song she loves—because she knows I love Lesley Gore. And I'm like, "No Way!" but I can't say that so I just say, "Yeah sure." Meanwhile This One's apparently supposed to be doing a lip sync to some Maria Callas song. But the thing is he's got this cabal...this coven of these twenty-five year old Opera-Buff-Monarchist types he hangs out with: The assistant to the Dean of Antiquated Studies at the University of Fa Fa Fa and Little Miss Fox Hunt and little Miss Cucumber Sandwiches and Little Lord Lady's Day At The Track. These are the kind of people who think Counter Culture is a yoghurt shop. Anyways. Story goes, the Monarchists put the kibosh on Maria Callas because apparently This One doesn't quite pass as a Maria Callas—or a Maria Anything I'd guess— and he was in danger of "embarrassing himself" which in the Opera-Buff-Monarchist world is second only to wearing brown shoes after six o'clock as something we "just can't have." So no Maria Callas—and This One has nothing to do at the Ceremony, so Kate suggests we get together on the Lesley Gore thing and I think, Great, this song is least opera-buff type song you can imagine and I'll work up this ridiculous dance and he'll be like "Perhaps not" and I'll be off the hook.

BRAD leaps out of his light.

Light snaps to the PAST.

Sound: the last chorus of "Sunshine, Lollipops."

BRAD finishes a ridiculous dance for BRIAN.

BRIAN: Well.

BRAD: Yeah.

BRIAN: It's quite energetic.

BRAD: Yeah, you know, I do a lot of yoga.

BRIAN: Right. It's a bit…

BRAD: Um hm?

BRIAN: Athletic.

BRAD: Do you find?

BRIAN: I've got a kind of a bad back.

BRAD: Ooo that can be dangerous.

BRIAN: And it's Sunday?

BRAD: Yeah Sunday.

BRIAN: I work on Monday morning.

BRAD: Me too. And it can't be a late night.

BRIAN: No.

BRAD: And it's going to be a long evening.

BRIAN: How do you mean?

BRAD: A full program.

BRIAN: Oh right, yes, of course.

BRAD: How did you think I meant it?

BRIAN: In no way…just… What do you think of Jessica?

BRAD: She's cool.

BRIAN: A little pushy, though, don't you find? For Kate?

BRAD: Pushy?

BRIAN: Opinionated.

BRAD: She has lots of opinions yeah—but so does Kate.

BRIAN: Oh that's a new thing.

BRAD: You don't like Jessica?

BRIAN: No just no you know.

BRAD: But she loves Kate.

BRIAN: Yeah she does love Kate.

            A beat.

BRAD: Are you still seeing…?

BRIAN: Gordon.

BRAD: Gordon?

BRIAN: No. Yes. No. Yes. No yes no yes no. Yes.

BRAD: Right.

BRIAN: On again off again.

BRAD: Right.

BRIAN: Basically it's a two-year relationship that's lasted for five years.

BRAD: *(Laughing.)* Been there buddy. So on now or off now?

BRIAN: Somewhere in between.

BRAD: Oh that hurts.

BRIAN: I like your jacket.

BRAD: Thanks.

BRIAN: It looks good on you.

BRAD: Thanks.

A beat.

BRIAN: So Sunday…

BRAD: Yeah Sunday…

BRIAN: What the heck.

BRAD: What?

BRIAN: Well it is for Kate and everything right?

BRAD: What about your back?

BRIAN: Oh. I was bluffing about my back, my back's fine. Strong like…horse.

BRAD: Oh.

BRIAN: So should we rehearse?

BRAD: What the heck.

BRAD takes off the jacket. Light slowly fades as:

See, sometimes we were happy.

BRIAN: No, sometimes we weren't sad.

Light continues to fade slightly then suddenly snaps to PLAY state (two specials.)

BRAD becomes RAY.

BRIAN becomes the DOCTOR.

DOCTOR: Good Morning Ray.

RAY: Good Morning Doc. So what's the verdict?

DOCTOR: The verdict?

RAY: Let's cut straight to the chase shall we?

DOCTOR: I came across one of those dream dictionaries we were talking about. I couldn't find "concrete boat" but it seems that boat represents a kind of rebirth.

RAY: What's the verdict?

DOCTOR: It's not good news.

            BRIAN steps downstage as the specials cross fade. He covers his tie, one arm across his chest and one hand at his throat becoming BRENDA.

BRENDA: But it's not the worse news, it could be worse.

RAY: Brenda?

BRENDA: Please Ray.

RAY: It's not good news—he said it's not good news.

BRENDA: But there are so many treatments—so many new treatments.

RAY: Brenda?

BRENDA: No.

RAY: No what?

BRENDA: I can't.

RAY: You can't what?

BRENDA: It's not healthy Ray. We're not healthy together. You're better off without me.

            BRENDA lifts her empty hand. RAY lifts the jacket he holds as if BRENDA has just handed it to him.

            I brought you back your jacket. I took it with me when I left, I thought I might want something to remind me of you.

RAY: But you don't?

BRENDA: But I don't.

RAY throws the jacket on the floor at BRENDA's feet.

RAY: Fuck you!

BRIAN drops his arms to his sides.

Light snaps to SHOW state.

BRAD: I don't buy it.

BRIAN: What?

BRAD: I don't buy it. So Brenda's just going to walk out on Ray?

BRIAN: Yes.

BRAD: Ray's dying and she doesn't care.

BRIAN: It's not about Brenda.

BRAD: It's all about Brenda now.

BRIAN lifts his arms to the BRENDA position.

Light snaps to PLAY state (one special).

Sound: a distant opera.

BRENDA: A word in my own defense, in which I struggle with cliches to try and describe the sensation of something suddenly going out. Not like a candle—not like a short sharp breeze and a pop and a slow glow down to nothing and then smoke. This is more like a shutter slamming or a cover closing—but not like that because the shutter and the cover indicate something within. This is the kind of going out where something collapses into itself and without a flutter turns to air. It is the feeling of something suddenly going out which is forever strangely linked to the image of a lambswool jacket lying on the floor.

BRAD speaks from the darkness.

BRAD:	You're going to have to do better than that.
	BRIAN drops his arms to his sides.
	Sound out.
	Light snaps to SHOW state.
BRIAN:	Better than what?
BRAD:	I'm not convinced.
BRIAN:	Of what?
BRAD:	The depth of her feeling.
BRIAN:	Excuse me?
BRAD:	And you're stretching the metaphor.
BRIAN:	The metaphor?
BRAD:	With your Jacket Thing.
BRIAN:	It's not my Jacket Thing.
BRAD:	Okay. The Jacket Thing.
BRIAN:	It's a different Jacket Thing.
BRAD:	It's "The Jacket Thing."
	BRIAN picks the jacket up from the floor and approaches BRAD.
BRIAN:	Brenda's leaving Ray because she can see what he's become.
BRAD:	Which is what?
BRIAN:	Which is just like everybody else.
BRAD:	There is no "everybody else."
BRIAN:	Oh that's deep.
BRAD:	To you maybe.

Light snap to the PAST.

Sound: distant heavy metal music.

BRIAN holds out the jacket to BRAD.

BRIAN: Take the jacket.

BRAD: I don't want the jacket.

BRIAN: Then why did you bring it up?

BRAD: I just asked if you were going to be wearing it tonight.

BRIAN: Wasn't that apparent? Seeing I was wearing it at the time.

BRAD: Forget it.

BRIAN: Do you want to wear the jacket?

BRAD: No. I don't care.

BRIAN: Wear it if you want to.

BRAD: No. It is my jacket.

BRIAN: Then wear it.

BRAD: You have lots of jackets.

BRIAN: So.

BRAD: I have two.

BRIAN: You never wear this jacket.

BRAD: Because you're always wearing it. You've been wearing it ever since we moved in together. Since before. You took it from my closet.

BRIAN: It was at the bottom of your laundry bag, you never wore it.

BRAD: I used to wear it all the time before you claimed it.

BRIAN: Claimed it? Oh please take the jacket. *(He throws the jacket at BRAD who catches it.)* What's your issue?

BRAD: I have no issue.

BRIAN: What's your issue?

BRAD: I don't like it when you wear my stuff.

BRIAN: What?

BRAD: It bugs me when you wear my stuff.

BRIAN: You're not serious.

BRAD: I know I know it's just a thing I don't know.

BRIAN: Okay okay I can accept that. It's petty but—and it certainly seems ironic coming from you.

BRAD: Ironic?

BRIAN: Ironic's a word.

BRAD: What's another word?

BRIAN: I thought we were supposed to end ownership.

BRAD: Nobody cares about the privatization of a jacket.

BRIAN: What's the difference?

BRAD: Maybe I have an emotional attachment to this jacket.

BRIAN: "Emotional attachment"…oh that's an interesting argument from the man who claims to be above sentiment.

BRAD: I made no "claim"—

BRIAN: Watch out or you'll be joining me as just another cog in the Patriarchal Industrial Bullshit Machine.

BRAD: I wasn't talking about you.

BRIAN: Bullshit Machine. You accuse my friends of being poseurs. It's the same damn thing. It's all just a persona.

BRAD: What is your issue?

BRIAN: Mister "Noam Chomsky."

BRAD: Mister "Lady Di."

BRIAN: Pardon me?

BRAD: Well if we're going to resort to name-calling.

BRIAN: Hypocrite.

BRAD throws the jacket on the floor at BRIAN's feet.

BRAD: Try it again. Defend yourself now. Go on.

BRIAN steps down into BRENDA's spot. He faces the audience put his arms in the BRENDA position.

BRENDA: A word in my own defence—

BRAD: What are you doing with your hands?

BRIAN: I'm hiding my tie.

BRAD: So she's wearing a tie.

BRIAN faces the audience.

Light: through the following, light cross fades slowly from SHOW to PLAY (one special for BRIAN, BRAD in darkness.)

BRIAN: A word in my own defence in which I struggle with clichés while searching for metaphors and come up with a grey lambswool jacket and something suddenly going out. A grey lambswool jacket lying on the floor and something suddenly...not like a candle, not like a short sharp breeze or a *(puts out a candle with his fingertips)* and a slow glow down to nothing and then smoke. This is sudden. And it leaves no trace. Just an unnameable emptiness—a name would give it too much weight—caused by something suddenly going out—and leaving behind nothing. Nothing, not even a nothing to hold up the nothing. And a grey lambswool jacket lying on the floor.

Light slowly fades to black.

BRAD begins speaking in the darkness. As he speaks the light fades up to SHOW state. BRAD is sitting on the floor.

BRAD: Is that how you felt about me? Empty? Not even a nothing to hold up a nothing? Is that why we were going to split up?

BRIAN picks up the jacket.

BRIAN: Why did you get so upset about the jacket?

BRAD: Because the first time we met you said I looked good in it.

BRIAN approaches BRAD. He stands over him looking down. BRIAN offers the jacket to BRAD.

You know there is such a thing as a concrete boat. People race them on a river in Missouri. I read about it in a magazine.

BRAD takes the jacket and puts it on.

Lots of people go to watch.

BRIAN: Hey Mister King.

Light snaps to PLAY state. One large special for LLOYD and RAY. BRAD becomes RAY. BRIAN becomes LLOYD.

RAY: Hey Lloyd.

LLOYD: Why are you sitting on our front lawn?

RAY: What?

LLOYD: You've been sitting on our front lawn for an hour.

RAY: I'm waiting for your Dad.

LLOYD: He's not my Dad.

RAY: Sorry. Terry.

LLOYD: He doesn't live here anymore.

RAY: Where is he?

LLOYD: I don't know. Hamilton maybe. Mrs. King's with him.

RAY: Are you telling me that Lloyd?

LLOYD: Didn't you know?

RAY: I knew.

LLOYD: Phew.

            LLOYD sits beside RAY. RAY stares at the moon.

            The grass is wet.

RAY: Is it?

LLOYD: Do you know the Bible?

RAY: Somewhat.

LLOYD: Okay, so there's Adam and Eve and they have kids, but who do their kids marry?

RAY: I don't know.

LLOYD: Seems weird. But you know the apostles right? How come when they wrote it they gave two of them the same name of Jacob. Why didn't they just give them different names so it wouldn't confuse people? Because somebody wrote it right?

RAY: I guess.

LLOYD: Is it made up or is it true?

RAY: It's whatever you want it to be I guess.

LLOYD: Oh. Because the same name thing kind of makes it
            seem like it is true. That that's how it really
            happened.

            Silence. LLOYD looks up at the moon with RAY.

            You know it's like everybody lives in this big circle
            and everybody wants to be in the centre of the
            circle but the centre of the circle is the smallest part.
            There's no way.

RAY: I'm dying.

LLOYD: Everybody's dying.

            RAY squeezes LLOYD's ear.

BRIAN: Ow!

BRAD: Poor Lloyd.

BRIAN: Poor Lloyd.

BRAD: Who's Lloyd supposed to be?

BRIAN: I think that's obvious isn't it?

BRAD: What's going to happen to Lloyd?

BRIAN: Oh he's going to grow up and become a computer
            geek and start an ingenious website and save the
            world and make a trillion dollars.

BRAD: Do you think?

BRIAN: I don't know. No. He just goes away when the play
            ends.

BRAD: That's sad.

BRIAN: That's life.

BRIAN gets up and walks away, out of the light. He takes up a position in the dark, parallel to BRAD but facing upstage.

Sound: crowd at a wedding reception.

Light cross fades to special for BRAD.

BRAD: Cheers cheers cheers and best wishes to Kate and Jessica on their happy day. It looks like I'm the last act of the evening—but unfortunately my partner seems to have gone AWOL—but fear not, in true showbiz tradition—whatever that is—everything's coming up roses and the show must go on and all that. So. Hit it Kate.

We hear "Sunshine Lollipops" in the background as BRAD addresses the audience.

The day before we had been rehearsing at This One's place and Little Miss Fox Hunt and Little Lord Lady's Day At The Track happened to be there and caught a bit of the act. Turns out they voted it "Silly" which in the Opera-Buff-Monarchist manifesto is a grade of the most horrific order and so This One acquits himself of the whole endeavor with not so much as a see-ya-later-sucker. A couple of nights later and I'm really pissed, in both senses of the word, and I dig up This One's phone number and decide to give him a piece of my irk.

Sound: a telephone rings. Light snaps up second special for BRIAN as he spins to face the audience.

BRIAN: Hello?

BRAD: Hey.

BRIAN: Hey!

BRAD: Yeah so hey.

BRIAN: I was just thinking about you.

BRAD: You were?

BRIAN: Yeah. I had a great time the other night.

BRAD: You did?

BRIAN: I'm sorry I had to leave.

BRAD: Why did you leave?

BRIAN: I told you I had to work in the morning.

BRAD: Yeah I know but—

BRIAN: Come over.

BRAD: Come over?

BRIAN: Come over.

BRAD: Uh. It's a bit late.

BRIAN: I want to make love to you.

BRAD: Oh. Okay. Oh. Okay. I guess.

BRIAN: Hurry.

Light: BRIAN's special out.

BRAD addresses the audience.

BRAD: Now, normally I wouldn't do that kind of thing but it was…Wednesday.

Light quick black.

Sound: a noisy doorbell.

Light snaps up to PAST. BRAD and BRIAN face one another.

Hey.

BRIAN: Oh hi.

Silence.

BRAD: Aren't you going to invite me in?

BRIAN: I'm kind of expecting someone.

BRAD: Yeah, me.

BRIAN: No, Gordon's coming over.

BRAD: Why didn't you tell me that?

BRIAN: Tell you that when?

BRAD: On the phone.

BRIAN: On the phone when?

BRAD: Twenty minutes ago.

BRIAN: Oh. Oh. Oh.

BRAD: Oh. Oh.

BRAD/BRIAN: Oh.

BRIAN: Well, do you want to come in?

BRAD: Well, that's why I'm here.

Sound: Sexy sexy music a la Barry White.

Light cross fades to deep red.

BRAD seductively takes off his jacket and playfully throws it at BRIAN. BRIAN catches it. BRAD approaches BRIAN slowly. BRAD loosens BRIAN's collar and tie then puts a hand on his chest, walking him backwards toward the chairs stage right. Just as it seems the men are about to kiss BRAD drops into the chair and BRIAN slips on the jacket as he steps to centre.

Sound: a busy bar.

Light: snaps to PLAY state (two specials).

BRAD becomes PAM ELLIS. BRIAN becomes RAY.

RAY: Ms. Ellis? Pam?

PAM: Pardon me?

RAY: Are you Lloyd's mother?

PAM: Yes.

RAY: I'm Raymond King. Brenda's husband.

PAM: Oh. Yes. Hello. Yes.

RAY: I just wanted to—

PAM: Offer condolences?

An uncomfortable beat.

Sorry. It's just that it's different for a woman. I guess. Or maybe not. How are you?

RAY: Oh, there's a lot going on these days. A lot to take my attention.

PAM: That's a good thing.

RAY: That's a good thing.

PAM: I didn't see it coming. Did you?

RAY: I...maybe.

PAM: Or I don't know...maybe I did. It's Lloyd really that I feel worse for. He'd really warmed to Terry. Since his father left it's been... But I'll be fine. It's Lloyd I worry about.

RAY: About Lloyd. I just wanted to let you know I've had my insurance policy placed in Lloyd's name.

PAM: Oh. You— Oh. Why?

RAY: You never know. Just in case. Accidents happen.

PAM: But why Lloyd?

RAY: Just to say—I'm sorry.

PAM: It's not your fault.

RAY: I'm just sorry that it had to happen.

PAM: Yes. Thanks.

RAY: Would you tell Lloyd something for me?

PAM: Yes?

RAY: Tell him the centre of the circle's not so great.

PAM: The centre of the circle?

RAY: Tell him you can't see the circle from the centre, and it's all about seeing the circle.

            A beat.

PAM: You know what my problem is Mr. King?

RAY: Ray.

PAM: My problem is I'm allergic to loneliness, and as poison as they may be to me, men are the only antidote I can find. But sometimes you've got to get sick to get better.

            RAY laughs.

            Can I buy you a drink, Ray?

RAY: Sure.

BRAD: *(To the audience.)* Another drunk woman.

BRIAN: Forget about that, what is this?

            Sound: out.

            Light snaps to SHOW state.

BRIAN takes a folded poster from his pocket and holds it up for the audience. The poster is a photograph of an expectant-looking BRAD listening for something coming on his left. Unnoticed by BRAD, on his right, BRIAN, leaning in, is about to stick his tongue in BRAD's ear.

What is this?

BRAD: The poster for the show.

BRIAN: There is no "show."

BRAD: There is now.

BRIAN: This is not acceptable.

BRAD: Why not?

BRIAN: Look at it. What's it supposed to be?

BRAD: *(Holding the photograph up for the audience.)* Well, there's me and I'm listening for something and there's you and you're about to stick your tongue in my ear.

BRIAN: Yes. I'm sure everybody's seen it.

BRAD: What's wrong with it?

BRIAN: Look at it. What's it supposed to mean? Look at me! I look like the embodiment of all evil?

BRAD: Well if the shoe fits…

BRIAN: Oh that's sweet.

BRAD: You did it for the photo.

BRIAN: I did it for the photo but I didn't know you were going to be looking all innocent like that.

BRAD: How was I supposed to look?

BRIAN: Not all innocent like that, you make me look terrible.

BRAD:	Well what would you like to look like?
BRIAN:	Obviously not the way you see me.
BRAD:	Oh here we go.
BRIAN:	Oh here we go where.
BRAD:	The village of image.
BRIAN:	Yes, well, it's my image.
BRAD:	Anyways...

Light snap to the PAST.

Sound: distant heavy metal.

BRAD:	Anyways...
BRIAN:	"Anyway!" "Anyway!" There is no such word as "Anyways!"
BRAD:	Don't! Don't correct me!
BRIAN:	I'm not it's just... You use it a thousand times a day. It's driving me to distraction.
BRAD:	Anyways! I just wish you could be yourself.
BRIAN:	What? What do you mean? What's that supposed to mean?
BRAD:	Forget it.
BRIAN:	No. What? What do you mean "yourself?" I am myself.
BRAD:	Fine.
BRIAN:	No. What's myself?
BRAD:	Like this ridiculous opera thing. You don't even like opera.
BRIAN:	I do so.

BRAD: You like Maria Callas. Maria Callas is not opera.
             Liking Maria Callas is like liking Barbra Steisand.

BRIAN: Take that back.

BRAD: You just think you should like opera because
             cultured people like opera—you think being an
             opera buff elevates you from your shameful
             working class background.

BRIAN: Anything else?

BRAD: You present yourself as this benign...this open
             minded...guardian of all things tasteful...

BRIAN: When in fact?

BRAD: When in fact you use your opinions—or the
             opinions you borrow from other people—

BRIAN: Oh!

BRAD: —in order to manipulate the situation to maintain
             control.

BRIAN: Well. If that's the way you feel...

BRAD: If that's the way I feel what?

BRIAN: Maybe we should just forget it.

BRAD: Forget what?

BRIAN: Nothing.

BRAD: Forget what?

BRIAN: Everything! I don't think we're working. I don't
             think we care anymore.

BRAD: What are you waiting for?

BRIAN: Exactly.

BRAD: No. What are you waiting for?

BRIAN: Something to happen.

                Light snaps to SHOW state.

                BRAD holds up the photograph once again.

BRAD: This One with the tongue represents something
                that happens. And That One, the innocent-looking
                one represents waiting for something to happen.
                And it sort of means…things sneak up on you.

BRIAN: Okay.

BRAD: Like this next part.

                Sound: a grandfather clock chimes.

                *Light snaps to PLAY state. (Two specials, BRAD in
                his, BRIAN just outside.)*

                BRAD becomes RAY's father, IRVING.

IRVING: Leave me be leave me be I'm not an invalid, I can
                get around just fine on my own steam thank you
                very much. Thug.

BRIAN: You don't have to play it like an "old man."

IRVING: I'll play it any way I want to. Thug! I can't find my
                thingamajig. I've been looking for it everywhere
                and I can't find it.

                BRIAN steps into his light as RAY.

RAY: Your which?

IRVING: My thingamajig—the whatsit with the thing—with
                the stuff in it. The brown one with the thing. You
                know.

RAY: No I don't Dad.

IRVING: The travelling box.

RAY: What?

IRVING: The travelling box. The box for travelling.

RAY: A suitcase?

IRVING: No. Is that…? Oh yes. Is that right? Yes I guess yes, suitcase.

            A beat.

            My hands are all gone funny.

RAY: What about it?

IRVING: What about what?

RAY: The suitcase.

IRVING: Oh no, I didn't bother with it since I couldn't find it. I won't be gone long anyway.

RAY: Where are you going?

IRVING: Nowhere. They've got thugs working here. Thugs. Guns and everything. One of them pulled a knife on me.

RAY: He was handing you a butter knife Dad. Dad, I have to tell you something. You won't be seeing me again.

IRVING: What's your name?

RAY: Raymond King. Ray.

IRVING: You ever kill a man Ray?

RAY: No.

IRVING: It's quite a thing. Had to of course had to. That was the thing. It was human lives at stake.

RAY: Yes.

IRVING: My uniform's gone. Took that too, the bastards. That was the thing. The uniforms. Because you just didn't think about it and you just put it on and that's what you wore and that's who you were and that was that. And what happened to the trains? They're always driving you around now. I don't like to be driven. But I like the trains. All over Germany that was a lovely train. And Spain.

Sound: distant trains.

Very high-class quality, high-class-type surroundings-type trains they've got in Spain. But Germany I liked better—because I've got a little Spanish you know, because of my French, I've got a little French, and Spanish is pretty close to French. But I haven't got a lick of German. So I preferred that. The German trains. Where I couldn't understand a word. There's nothing better really. On the train and people all around you and you know they're not talking to you—and even if they were, all you've got to do is *(shrugs shoulders)* and pretty soon you're left to yourself and the lovely little towns and the countryside changing and changing and the trains and the trains…I keep waiting for something to happen. I keep waiting and waiting for something to happen.

RAY: I know.

Sound: little girls playing.

IRVING: My little skipping girls have all gone home.

RAY: Who?

IRVING: From the lawn. Your Mom made cookies but the girls were gone. There's lots left if you want some. Extra-raisin kind.

RAY: I better go now Dad.

IRVING: What's your name?

RAY looks at IRVING.

RAY: Raymond King.

         Silence.

         BRAD faces BRIAN.

BRAD: Now what?

BRIAN: Ray leaves his father and he gets into his blue Mercedes.

BRAD: And you'll be Ray?

BRIAN: And I'll be Ray.

BRAD: And I'm me?

BRIAN: Yes.

         BRAD and BRIAN address the audience.

BRAD: You've got to run some errands.

RAY: What it comes down to now is intention.

BRAD: Pick up a prescription for somebody's migraine. Toilet paper. Exchange some tickets. The usual.

RAY: What it comes down to now is the difference between intention and accident.

BRAD: A usual day. Not a bad day just a usual day.

RAY: In my big powerful fast machine.

BRAD: In the car driving along. Aware of the machinery— big powerful fast machines passing a lot of other big powerful fast machines driven by people about whose sobriety nor mental state you know nothing. That thought's a bit heavy.

RAY: Just another accident.

BRAD: You go for the radio.

RAY: Just like everything.

BRAD:	Crap.
RAY:	Just like everything.
BRAD:	Crap.
RAY:	Just like everything.
BRAD:	More crap.
RAY:	I wish I'd said "I'm sorry" more.
BRAD:	Crap.
RAY:	I wish I'd said "I know" less.
BRAD:	Something familiar.
RAY:	I wish I never said "nothing" when I meant something.
BRAD:	Crap.
RAY:	And I'm glad my Mother's gone…
BRAD:	Back to something familiar.
RAY:	… and that my father won't know the difference.
BRAD:	Where was it?
RAY:	And Brenda will sing at my funeral…
BRAD:	Can't find it.
RAY:	… and Terry will love her…
BRAD:	One-oh-one point what?
RAY:	… and Lloyd will be fine…
BRAD:	Or after?
RAY:	… and Pam is a beautiful woman…
BRAD:	No, before the sports, after the metal.

RAY: ... and Miles is just me but lost sooner.

BRAD: There it is.

RAY: And just a quick jerk of the wheel.

BRAD: And in that moment...

RAY: Just like everything else.

BRAD: It's the headlights of the blue Mercedes.

RAY: Just another accident.

                *RAY closes his eyes, seeing what BRAD is
                describing.*

BRAD: An incredible vortex of slow motion and silence.
                Spinning through time, lighter than air,
                weightless. Weightless and perfectly calm. You
                look out the window and it's filled with sky—the
                tops of buildings and trees and electrical wires
                slowly moving past, and as they do they turn to
                smoke. A thick black smoke that takes a moment to
                disperse. Everything turns to smoke then holds its
                shape for a moment then drifts away from itself.
                The leaves, the wires, the trees, the buildings. And
                you feel sad that it's going but at the same time you
                feel this blissful peace at being able to witness it go
                away. And you think: "This is what it's like to die."
                But no, then you realize: "No...

                RAY opens his eyes.

                No, this is what it's like to be alive." And then...

RAY: And then you're gone.

BRAD: ... you're gone.

                Light slowly fades to black.

                *We wait in the blackout for some time, as if the play
                is over. Just before the audience applauds and in the
                blackout BRAD speaks.*

Do you really find this a satisfying ending?

BRIAN: What?

BRAD: I just think there are probably a few more options.

BRIAN: For God's sake.

BRAD: Do you mind?

BRIAN: Whatever.

> *Light snaps to PERFORMANCE state.*
>
> *BRAD addresses the audience as he sets the two chairs centre.*

BRAD: First date. My idea. We go to a play.

BRIAN: It was hardly a play.

BRAD: It was this performance thing Kate was putting on.

BRIAN: What was that anyway?

BRAD: It was interesting.

BRIAN: Faint praise.

BRAD: But it's this thing where we're supposed to arrive at nine, and we get there and there's nobody else around except the box office guy—so he sells us our tickets and he sends us around the back of the building. This One's already complaining.

BRIAN: I was not, I was on my best behaviour.

BRAD: Everything's relative. Anyway. We go in the back door and it's this big empty warehouse space and these bright lights.

BRIAN: Blinding.

BRAD: And in the middle of the space there are these two chairs. I can tell immediately that This One wants to bolt.

BRIAN: But I don't.

BRAD: But he doesn't and we sit in the chairs and nothing's happening and nothing's happening and then we hear somebody laugh. So we look around and about thirty metres out past the lights is the audience of—

BRIAN: Thousands!

BRAD: Fifty maybe. And first it's like "What the hell is going on?" and then it's like "Oh my God they think we're the show!"

BRIAN: Oh my God.

BRAD: And then it got kind of weird because we don't know what to do.

BRIAN: So we just sit there.

BRAD: So we just sit there and pretty soon they're thinking "They don't know what they're doing."

            A long silence as BRAD and BRIAN find themselves back in the strange, uncomfortable moment. BRAD is loving it, BRIAN is mortified.

BRIAN: And then it got kind of tense.

BRAD: And then it got kind of nice.

BRIAN: It did?

BRAD: I took your hand.

            BRAD takes BRIAN's hand.

BRIAN: Yes, you did.

BRAD: Which was like I might as well have kissed him full on the mouth This One is so in the closet.

BRIAN: *(Pulling his hand away.)* I am not.

BRAD: Anyway.

BRIAN: Anyways.

            BRIAN puts his hand on BRAD's leg for a moment.

            It was nice. *(Taking his hand away.)* Although once I
            got to know you I was convinced it was just
            another one of your radical political statements.

BRAD: *(Honestly; looking at BRIAN.)* Well it wasn't.

            Beat. BRIAN looks away.

BRIAN: Well, I guess it's an option for an ending, but it's a
            bit on the sentimental side.

BRAD: You ain't seen nothing yet. Hit it Kate!

            Sound: "Sunshine Lollipops" plays from the top.

            *BRAD grabs the chairs and rushes them back to
            their opening position. He rushes back and begins
            the dance. BRIAN is horrified, slowly he joins it
            until they both dance the ridiculous dance, laughing
            and loving it.*

            *The dance ends. BRIAN faces the audience as if to
            take a bow. BRAD indicates to the audience that it's
            not over yet. BRIAN looks at BRAD. BRAD moves
            to step off the stage.*

BRIAN: Where are you going?

BRAD: To pick up your prescription.

            Light slow fades to SHOW state.

            BRIAN pauses:

BRIAN: Didn't you do that yet?

BRAD: I'm doing it now.

BRIAN: God.

BRAD: What?

BRIAN: Nothing.

BRAD: Good. Do we need anything else?

BRIAN: Yes, toilet paper for the how manyeth time.

BRAD: Right right right.

BRIAN: And could you please exchange those tickets.

BRAD: I'll do it tomorrow.

BRIAN: You said that last week.

BRAD: We've exchanged them three times already.

BRIAN: Fine, we'll give them away.

BRAD: Keep a schedule.

BRIAN: I do.

BRAD: Write it down!

BRIAN: I did.

BRAD: Pin the list to your mitten!

BRIAN: Well then don't.

BRAD: No fine fine.

BRIAN: Try Saturday.

BRAD: A change charge and an upgrade?

BRIAN: Fine.

BRAD: Tuesday?

BRIAN: No. Kate's bringing Karen over to meet us on Tuesday.

BRAD: We met Karen already.

BRIAN: "Privately."

BRAD: Great.

BRIAN: She's your friend.

BRAD: What's that supposed to mean?

BRIAN: She doesn't call me any more.

BRAD: You can't pick up the phone?

BRIAN: Why is that my fault? Why is everything always my fault?

BRAD: We have to talk.

BRIAN: I have a migraine.

BRAD: You always have a migraine.

BRIAN: We'll talk when you get back.

BRAD: Fine.

BRIAN: Try Wednesday.

BRAD: Wednesday.

BRIAN and
BRAD: Next Wednesday.

BRIAN: And shampoo.

BRAD: And shampoo.

> *BRAD moves to leave again.*

BRIAN: How are you getting there?

BRAD: I'm riding my bike.

BRIAN: To the plaza?

BRAD: Sure.

BRIAN: And the theatre?

BRAD: Yeah.

BRIAN: You're not going to go to the theatre if you take your bicycle.

BRAD: I need the exercise.

BRIAN: I just want to get this dealt with.

BRAD: I'm dealing with it.

BRIAN: Here it's going to rain anyway, take my car.

            BRIAN reaches into his pocket and mimes throwing keys to BRAD. BRAD pretends to catch the keys he has been hiding in his hand. BRAD moves to step off the stage. He turns back.

            Prescription, toilet paper, tickets and...?

BRIAN: You've helped me to see the beauty in people and you've been a really good friend.

BRAD: *(Mildly scolding.)* That's not how it went.

BRIAN: Shampoo.

BRAD: Shampoo.

            BRAD steps off the stage and walks through the audience toward the door of the theatre.

BRIAN: And not the cheap shit.

BRAD: Right right.

            BRIAN moves to centre.

            Light slowly fades down to special on BRIAN as at top of play.

            BRAD exits the theatre slamming the door.

            Sound: footsteps on a gravel driveway, a car door opening, a car door shutting, a car starting, a car pulling out of the driveway, driving, driving, driving. BRIAN speaks against the sound.

BRIAN: Of course another option would be...for an
                ending...would be to take it all full circle. To end
                up back where we began. People like a package.
                People like a tidy package. So... So... Ray leaves
                his father and he gets in his car and instead he goes
                back to the Doctor. And Ray says: "Hey Doc." And
                the Doctor says: "How are you Ray?" And... And
                then Ray says: "How long have I got Doc?" No,
                let's give him a name. Charlie. And Ray says:
                "How long have I got Charlie?" And the Doctor
                says: "I can't answer that question Ray" And Ray
                says...Ray says: "Come on Charlie we've got the
                verdict what's the sentence?"

                Sound: driving, driving, driving.

BRIAN: And the Doctor says: "I can't—" and Ray inter-
                rupts him and he says: "I need a number Charlie, a
                number." And the Doctor says: "Well at this point
                it could happen at any time. We could be talking
                about days or weeks. Maybe months. Possibly as
                long as thirty or forty years. But the bottom line is
                each day could potentially be your last and so I
                would advise you to start living your life accord-
                ingly." And then a look of confusion which slowly
                becomes understanding then relief. Ray looks out
                at the audience —almost smiling but still unsure.
                Then he steps off the stage, through the audience,
                out the door, into the world, ready to begin his new
                life.

                Sound: a signal light. A radio turned on, bad music,
                news, sports, bad music, the Maria Callas aria,
                news, a search to find the aria again, finally finding
                the aria. A long sustained note over tires squealing.
                And huge explosive impact. Accident scene sounds.
                Female voices shrieking: "Oh my God! What
                happened? The blue Mercedes swerved right into
                him." etc. Sirens. Police band radio. Finally the aria
                alone.

BRIAN takes off the jacket and holds it. He waits for the final phrase and completion of the aria. It stops in a pause, not finishing.

BRIAN holds the jacket out before him.

BRIAN: But why are we talking about endings anyway? Some things end. But some things just stop.

BRIAN drops the jacket on the floor where he picked it up at the top of the show. BRIAN turns and leaves the stage. Just as he disappears from view the aria finishes.

Light fades to spot on jacket then black with end of aria.

The End